mbroidery on
parchment paper

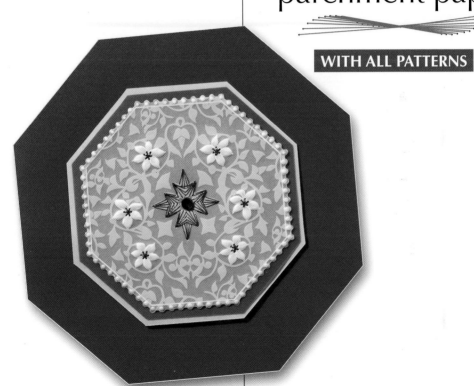

WITH ALL PATTERNS

Gerti Hofman

FORTE PUBLISHERS

Contents

ISBN 90 5877 512 7

This is a publication from
Forte Publishers BV
P.O. Box 1394
3500 BJ Utrecht
The Netherlands

For more information about the creative books available from
Forte Uitgevers:
www.forteuitgevers.nl

Final editing: Gina Kors-Lambers, Steenwijk, the Netherlands
Photography and digital image editing:
Fotografie Gerhard Witteveen, Apeldoorn, the Netherlands
Cover and inner design:
BADE creatieve communicatie, Baarn, the Netherlands
Translation: Michael Ford, TextCase, Hilversum, the Netherlands

Pergamano® is the brand name under which books and materials for parchment crafting are sold.

Preface

In this book, I have used parchment paper and parchment vellum, which are
both available in many different colours and in many different designs, as
well as embroidery thread, which is also available in many attractive colours.
These two materials make an excellent combination.
The subtle, transparent effect of parchment paper and parchment vellum
combined with elegant embroidery stitches gives very surprising results.

The patterns in this book are shapes from nature in a stylized form
combined with stylish, geometric shapes. These patterns have then
been decorated with shiny embroidery thread on parchment paper
and parchment vellum to give a very tasteful result.

Gerti

Techniques

Pricking

Always make a copy of the pattern first. Parchment paper is transparent and can be stuck on the pattern so that you can see the pattern through the paper.

If you have to prick through two or more layers, then always prick one layer first. Next, place this layer on top of the other layers and prick the pattern through all of the other layers using the holes you pricked in the first layer.

Embroidering

Use a very fine embroidery needle, so that the holes do not become too large. Do not use tape to attach the embroidery thread. Since the parchment paper is transparent, it will show through the paper, even when using two layers. It is best to attach the thread by sewing it into the embroidery at the back of the card.

Stem stitch

The stem stitch in the most common stitch used in this book. Examples of the other stitches used in this book are given with the pattern.

Tassel

Step 1

Wind a 100 cm long thread 5 or 6 times around four fingers and hold it with your thumb (part 1). Place this on the table. Take a 70 cm long thread and tie the ends together.

Step 2

Insert an embossing pen through the loop under the knot. Insert your forefinger through the other side of the loop and wind the loop tightly around your finger. Slide this loop also over the embossing pen (part 2). Slide part 1 through both loops of part 2 to create a T-shape.

Place it on the table with the long end facing away from you. Make a loop using a different coloured thread (18 cm) and place the loop 2 cm above the knot with the ends facing downwards. Fold the threads of part 1 and the loop downwards to make a tassel.

Step 3

Take a 20 cm long thread and wind it 5 or 6 times tightly around the tassel and push the start and end of the thread through the coloured thread. Pull the ends of the coloured thread so that the threads are pulled through the loop.

Step 4

Tie a knot above the tassel and cut the ends off.

Step-by-step

Step 1

Step 2

Step 3

Step 4

Materials

- Parchment paper and parchment vellum
- Felt embossing pad (1413)
- Embossing pen - extra fine ball (11071)
- Embossing pen - small ball (11011)
- Embossing pen - large ball (11021)
- Perga spray (1129)
- Perga kit (1411)
- Mapping pen (1420)
- Fine embroidery needle
- Embroidery thread

Materials for pricking

- Pergamano cutting mat (1418)
  This mat is thin so that the perforations are not too deep to give nice small holes.
- Pergamano 1-needle pen (11041)
  This perforating tool makes a small hole.
- Pergamano 1-needle pen - extra large (1137)
  This perforating tool makes a large hole, so that a number of threads can be thread through the hole.

Blossom

Card with blossom

What you need

- *Lilac purple fantasy parchment (1604)*
- *Dotted parchment vellum (1643)*
- *White paper*
- *Sulky thread: white metallic prism (7021)*
- *Silver, holographic line stickers*
- *White Tinta ink (01T) and blocks of foam tape (1201)*

Instructions

General instructions

This card is made from lilac purple fantasy parchment and has four extra sheets stuck on the front. The first extra sheet is made from white paper, the second extra sheet is made from dotted parchment vellum and the third and fourth extra sheets are made from lilac purple fantasy parchment. Cut all the pieces to the right size.

Tracing

Use white Tinta ink (01T) to trace the flowers and the branches on the fourth extra sheet.

Embossing

Emboss the flowers and the branch.

Pricking

Use the 1-needle pen to prick the pattern. Use Perga spray to stick the fourth extra sheet to the third extra sheet and prick the holes again.

Embroidering

Embroider outwards from the holes around the heart of the flower.

Finishing

Fold the card. Use Perga spray to stick the first and second extra sheets to the card.
Use foam tape to stick the third and fourth extra sheets to the card. Add some silver, peel-off line stickers.

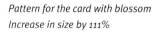

Pattern for the card with blossom
Increase in size by 111%

 *Embroidery*

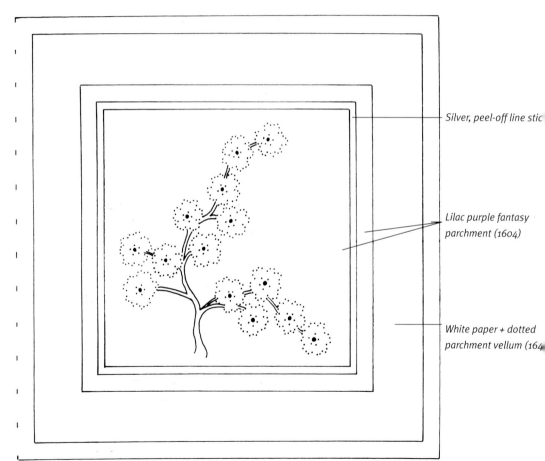

Silver, peel-off line stic

Lilac purple fantasy parchment (1604)

White paper + dotted parchment vellum (164

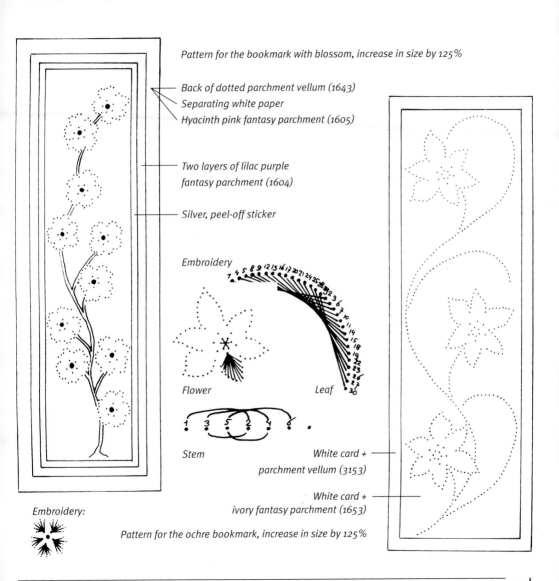

Pattern for the bookmark with blossom, increase in size by 125%

Back of dotted parchment vellum (1643)
Separating white paper
Hyacinth pink fantasy parchment (1605)

Two layers of lilac purple
fantasy parchment (1604)

Silver, peel-off sticker

Embroidery

Flower

Leaf

Stem

White card +
parchment vellum (3153)

White card +
ivory fantasy parchment (1653)

Embroidery:

Pattern for the ochre bookmark, increase in size by 125%

Bookmark with blossom

What you need
- Hyacinth pink fantasy parchment (1605)
- Lilac purple fantasy parchment (1604)
- Dotted parchment vellum (1643)
- White paper
- Sulky thread: white metallic prism (7021)
- Silver, holographic line stickers and 10 dots (841)
- White Tinta ink 01T (1201)
- Pergamano bookmark cover (1174)
- Silver decorative thread

Instructions

General instructions
The front of the bookmark is made from hyacinth pink fantasy parchment. The bookmark has two extra sheets on the front made from lilac purple fantasy parchment. The back is made from white paper and dotted parchment vellum. Cut all the pieces to the right size.

Tracing
Use white Tinta ink (01T) to trace the branch on the second extra sheet.

Embossing
Emboss the branch.

Pricking
Use the 1-needle pen to prick the pattern. Use Perga spray to stick the first extra sheet behind the second extra sheet and prick the holes again.

Embroidering
Embroider outwards from the holes around the heart of the flower.

Finishing
Use Perga spray to stick all the parts together as shown in the photograph. Add the silver, peel-off line stickers. Slide it into the bookmark cover and cut the cover so that it is 16.5 cm long. Use a hole punch to make a hole in the middle of the open end of the cover and tie a tassel to it (see Step-by-step).

Ochre

Ochre bookmark

What you need

- *Ivory fantasy parchment (1652)*
- *Soft orange vellum (3153)*
- *White card (cArt-us)*
- *Madeira embroidery thread - ochre (1372),*
  soft yellow (1270) and brass (1173)
- *Pergamano bookmark cover (1174)*
- *Gold decorative thread*

Instructions

General instructions
The bookmark is made from white card with soft orange vellum stuck on top. It has two extra sheets stuck to the front. The first extra sheet is made from white card and the second extra sheet is made from ivory fantasy parchment. First, cut all the pieces to the right size.

Pricking
Use a 1-needle pen to prick the pattern in the second extra sheet. Use Perga spray to stick the second extra sheet on the first extra sheet and prick the holes again.

Embroidering
Embroider the pattern.

Finishing
Use Perga spray to stick all the parts together as shown in the photograph. Slide it into the bookmark cover and cut the cover so that it is 16.5 cm long. Use a hole punch to make a hole in the middle of the open end of the cover and tie a tassel to it (see Step-by-step).

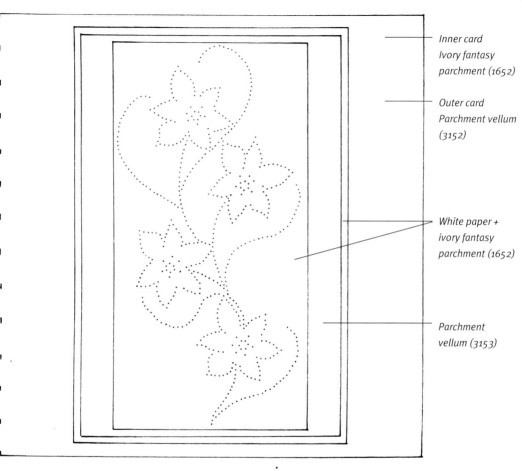

Inner card
Ivory fantasy
parchment (1652)

Outer card
Parchment vellum
(3152)

White paper +
ivory fantasy
parchment (1652)

Parchment
vellum (3153)

Pattern for the ochre flower card
Increase in size by 111%

• *Embroidery: stem*

Embroidery: flower

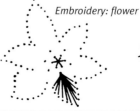

Embroidery: leaf

Ochre flower card

What you need

- *Ivory fantasy parchment (1652)*
- *Ochre vellum (3152)*
- *Soft orange vellum (3153)*
- *White card (cArt-us)*
- *Double-sided adhesive tape*
- *Madeira embroidery thread - ochre (1372), soft yellow (1270) and brass (1173)*

Instructions

General instructions

The inner card is made from ivory fantasy parchment and the outer card is made from ochre vellum. The card has five extra sheets stuck on the front. The first and fourth extra sheets are made from white card, the second and fifth extra sheets are made from ivory fantasy parchment and the third extra sheet is made from soft orange vellum. First, cut all the pieces to the right size first.

Pricking

Use a 1-needle pen to prick the pattern in the fifth extra sheet. Use Perga spray to stick the fifth extra sheet on the fourth extra sheet and prick the holes again.

Embroidering

Embroider the pattern.

Finishing

Fold the inner card and the outer card and use a soft yellow embroidery thread to stitch them together along the line of the fold. Use Perga spray to stick all the extra sheets together as shown in the photograph and then use narrow strips of double-sided adhesive tape to stick these on the front of the outer card.

Fuchsias

Pattern for fuchsia on white
Increase in size by 111%

Embroidery:

● = emboss

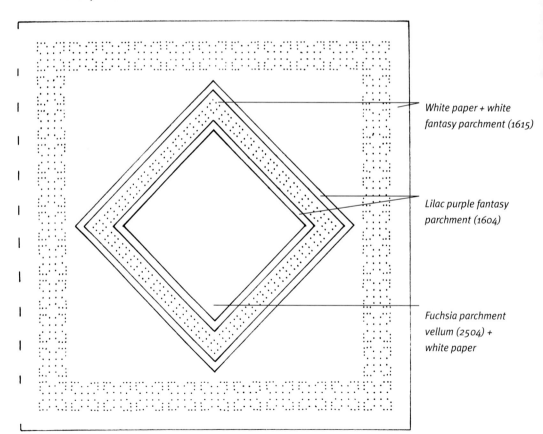

White paper + white
fantasy parchment (1615)

Lilac purple fantasy
parchment (1604)

Fuchsia parchment
vellum (2504) +
white paper

Fuchsia on white

What you need

- Lilac purple fantasy parchment (1604)
- White fantasy parchment (1651)
- Fuchsia parchment vellum (2504)
- Sulky thread: pink metallic (7012)
- Sulky thread: fuchsia metallic (7055)
- Double-sided adhesive tape

Instructions

General instructions

The inner card and the outer card are made from white fantasy parchment. The card has six extra sheets stuck on the front. The first and fourth extra sheets are made from lilac purple fantasy parchment, the second and fifth extra sheets are made from white paper, the third extra sheet is made from white fantasy parchment and the sixth extra sheet is made from fuchsia parchment vellum. Cut all the pieces to the right size.

Pricking

Prick the pattern in the outer card and the third extra sheet. Use Perga spray to stick the third extra sheet on the second extra sheet and prick the holes again.

Embossing

Emboss small dots along the border in the middle of the perforated shapes (see the pattern).

Embroidering

Embroider the pattern. Embroider the shapes along the outside border outwards from the holes in the middle of the shape.

Finishing

Fold the inner card and the outer card and use an embroidery thread to stitch them together along the line of the fold. Use Perga spray to stick all the extra sheets together in the right order and use double-sided adhesive tape to stick them on the card.

Pattern for fuchsia on purple
Increase in size by 111%

Embroidery:

● = emboss

Lilac purple fantasy parchment (1604)

White fantasy parchment (1651) + white paper

Fuchsia parchment vellum (2504) + white paper

Silver, peel-off line sticker

Fuchsia on purple

What you need

- *Lilac purple fantasy parchment (1604)*
- *White fantasy parchment (1651)*
- *Fuchsia parchment vellum (2504)*
- *Sulky thread: metallic prism white (7021)*
- *Silver, peel-off line stickers (842)*
- *Double-sided adhesive tape*

Instructions

General instructions
The outer card is made from lilac purple fantasy parchment and the inner card is made from white fantasy parchment. The card has five extra sheets stuck on the front. The first and fourth extra sheets are made from white paper, the second extra sheet is made from white fantasy parchment, the third extra sheet is made from lilac purple fantasy parchment and the fifth extra sheet is made from fuchsia parchment vellum. Cut all the pieces to the right size.

Pricking
Prick the pattern in the outer card.

Embossing
Emboss small dots along the border in the middle of the perforated shapes (see the pattern).

Embroidering
Embroider the pattern. Embroider outwards from the holes in the middle of the shape.

Finishing
Fold the inner card and the outer card and use an embroidery thread to stitch them together along the line of the fold. Use Perga spray to stick all the extra sheets together in the right order and use double-sided adhesive tape to stick them on the card. Add the silver, peel-off line stickers.

Embroidery:

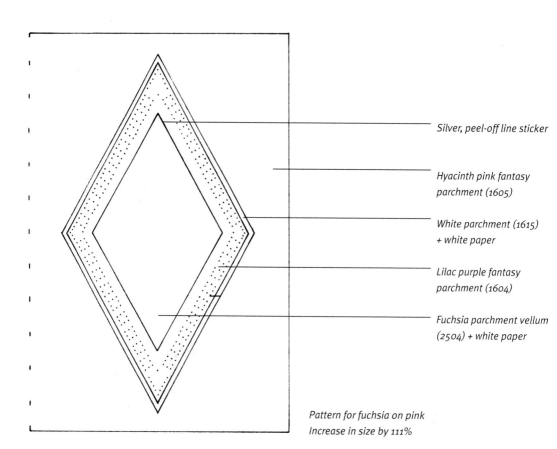

Silver, peel-off line sticker

Hyacinth pink fantasy
parchment (1605)

White parchment (1615)
+ white paper

Lilac purple fantasy
parchment (1604)

Fuchsia parchment vellum
(2504) + white paper

Pattern for fuchsia on pink
Increase in size by 111%

Fuchsia on pink

Instructions

General instructions
The outer card is made from hyacinth pink fantasy parchment and the inner card is made from white fantasy parchment. The card has five extra sheets stuck on the front. The first and fourth extra sheets are made from white paper, the second extra sheet is made from white fantasy parchment, the third extra sheet is made from lilac purple fantasy parchment and the fifth extra sheet is made from fuchsia parchment vellum. Cut all the pieces to the right size.

Pricking
Prick the pattern in the third extra sheet.

Embroidering
Embroider the pattern.

Finishing
Fold the inner card and the outer card and use an embroidery thread to stitch them together along the line of the fold. Use Perga spray to stick all the extra sheets together in the right order and use double-sided adhesive tape to stick them on the card. Add the silver, peel-off line stickers.

What you need
- Hyacinth pink fantasy parchment (1605)
- Lilac purple fantasy parchment (1604)
- White fantasy parchment (1651)
- Fuchsia parchment vellum (2504)
- Sulky thread: white metallic prism (7021)
- Silver, peel-off line stickers (842)
- Double-sided adhesive tape

Octagonal card

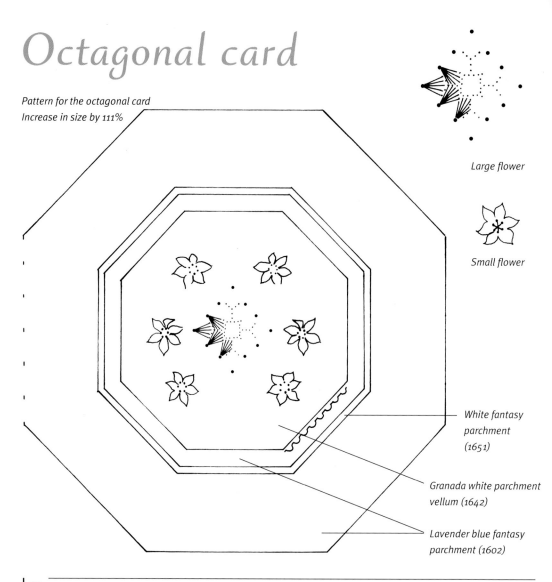

Pattern for the octagonal card
Increase in size by 111%

Large flower

Small flower

White fantasy
parchment
(1651)

Granada white parchment
vellum (1642)

Lavender blue fantasy
parchment (1602)

Octagonal card

What you need
- White fantasy parchment (1651)
- Lavender blue fantasy parchment (1602)
- Granada white vellum (1642)
- Sulky thread: metallic blue (7016)
- White Tinta ink 01T (1201)
- Fiskars border figure scissors: puzzle
- Make Me adhesive stones: dark blue

Instructions

General instructions
This card is made from lavender blue fantasy parchment. The card has three extra sheets stuck on the front. The first extra sheet is made from white fantasy parchment, the second extra sheet is made from lavender blue fantasy parchment and the third extra sheet is made from Granada white vellum. Cut all the pieces to the right size.

Tracing
Use white Tinta ink (01T) to trace the outline and the six flowers on the third extra sheet.

Embossing
Emboss the leaves of the six flowers and the outline. Use the border figure scissors to cut around the outline. Emboss small dots around

Pricking
Use the 1-needle pen to prick the pattern in the third extra sheet. Use Perga spray to stick the third extra sheet on the second extra sheet and prick the holes again.

Embroidering
Embroider the pattern.

Finishing
Fold the card. Use Perga spray to stick the extra sheets on the card and decorate the card with the blue adhesive stone.

Pastel with flowers

Stem stitch

Detail of the flower in the bottom left-hand corner

Detail of the flower in the top right-hand corner

Stripped pastel vellum (2502)
Separating sheet + inner card of white fantasy parchment (1651)

Pattern for pastel with flowers
Increase in size by 11%

Pastel with flowers

Instructions

General instructions
The inner card is made from white fantasy parchment and the outer card is made from stripped pastel vellum.

Tracing
Use white Tinta ink (01T) to draw the double outline on the inner card.

Embossing
Emboss the double outline.

Pricking
Prick the pattern in the outer card.

Embroidering
Embroider the pattern using the stem stitch.

Finishing
Fold the cards. Use an embroidery thread to stitch the cards together along the line of the fold.

What you need
- White fantasy parchment (1651)
- Stripped pastel vellum (2502)
- White Tinta ink 01T (1201)
- Sulky thread: purple metallic (7050)

Ice blue

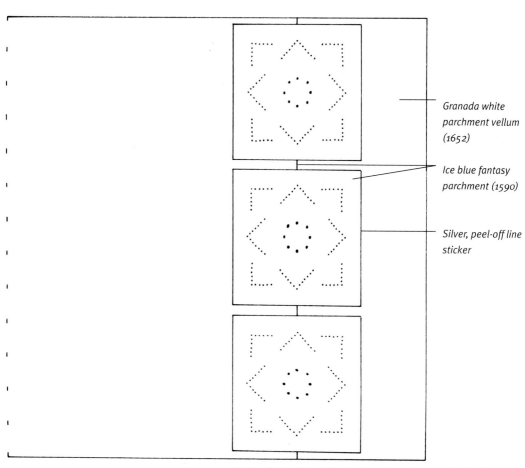

Granada white parchment vellum (1652)

Ice blue fantasy parchment (1590)

Silver, peel-off line sticker

Pattern for ice blue with adhesive stones. Increase in size by 111%

Ice blue with adhesive stones

What you need

- Ice blue fantasy parchment (1590)
- White fantasy parchment (1651)
- Granada white parchment vellum (1652)
- Sulky thread: silver/pink/light blue metallic
- Silver, peel-off line stickers (842)
- Make Me adhesive stones: light blue
- Double-sided adhesive tape

Instructions

General instructions

The outer card is made from ice blue fantasy parchment and the inner card is made from white fantasy parchment. The card has seven extra sheets stuck on the front. The first, rectangular, extra sheet is made from Granada white parchment vellum and the other six, square, extra sheets are made from ice blue fantasy parchment. Cut all the pieces to the right size.

Pricking

Use a 1-needle pen to prick the pattern in the three squares. Use Perga spray to stick the three squares to the other three squares and prick the holes again.

Embroidering

Embroider the pattern. Embroider outwards from the holes in the middle of the shape.

Finishing

Fold the inner card and the outer card and use an embroidery thread to stitch them together along the line of the fold. Use Perga spray to stick the first extra sheet to the card. Use narrow strips of double-sided adhesive tape to stick the three squares on the card. Add some silver, peel-off line stickers and some adhesive stones.

Pattern for ice blue with squares
Increase in size by 111%

Embroidery: flower

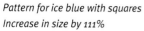
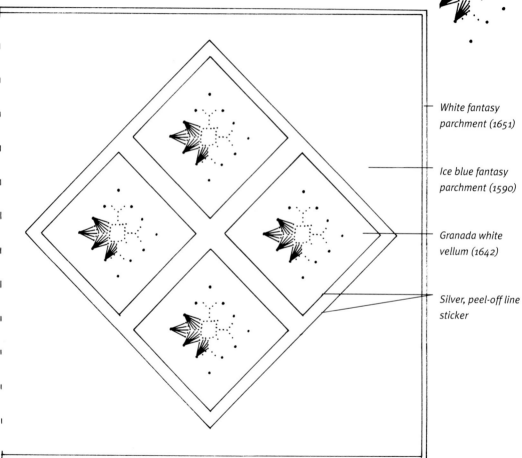

White fantasy parchment (1651)

Ice blue fantasy parchment (1590)

Granada white vellum (1642)

Silver, peel-off line sticker

Ice blue with squares

Instructions

General instructions

The outer card is made from ice blue fantasy parchment and the inner card is made from white fantasy parchment. The card has four extra sheets stuck on the front made from Granada white parchment vellum. Cut all the pieces to the right size. Cut the squares out of the ice blue card and cut the squares out of the vellum 1 cm bigger so that the flower/star fits exactly in the middle.

Pricking

Use a 1-needle pen to prick the pattern in the four squares.

Embroidering

Embroider the pattern. Embroider from the outer holes towards the middle.

Finishing

Fold the inner card and the outer card and use an embroidery thread to stitch them together along the line of the fold. Use narrow strips (1 mm) of double-sided adhesive tape to stick the four squares on the card. Stick silver, peel-off line stickers over the top. Add the other line stickers and the four silver dots.

What you need

- Ice blue fantasy parchment (1590)
- White fantasy parchment (1651)
- Granada white parchment vellum (1652)
- Sulky thread: sliver metallic light blue (145-8053)
- Silver, peel-off line stickers (842)
- Double-sided adhesive tape

Gold on ivory

Pattern for three stars
Increase in size by 111%

Ivory fantasy parchment (1653) ⌐

Gold vellum (1611)⌐

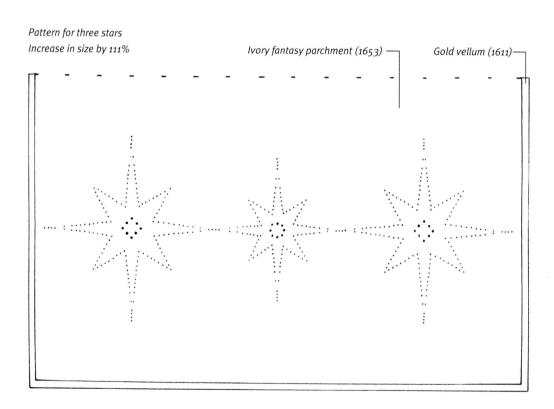

Three stars

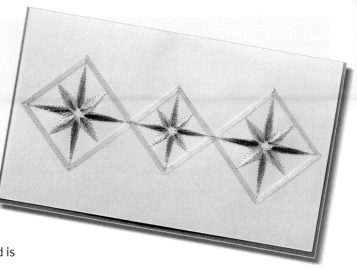

What you need

- *Ivory fantasy parchment (1653)*
- *White fantasy parchment (1651)*
- *Gold parchment vellum (1611)*
- *Sulky thread: gold metallic*

Instructions

General instructions
The outer card is made from ivory fantasy parchment and the inner card is made from gold parchment vellum. The card has a separating sheet made from ivory parchment vellum. Cut all the pieces to the right size.

Pricking
Fold the outer card and then fold it open again. Prick the pattern in the front of the outer card. Use Perga spray to stick the separating sheet behind the front of the outer card and prick the holes again.

Embroidering
First, embroider the stars from the holes in the middle towards the outside and then the lines of the squares around the stars.

Finishing
Fold the inner card and the outer card and use an embroidery thread to stitch them together along the line of the fold.

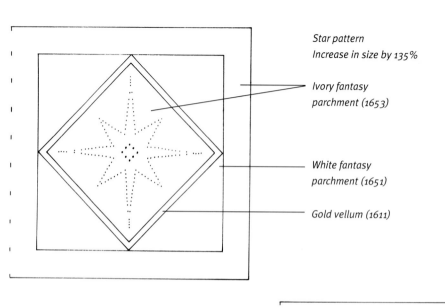

Star pattern
Increase in size by 135%

Ivory fantasy
parchment (1653)

White fantasy
parchment (1651)

Gold vellum (1611)

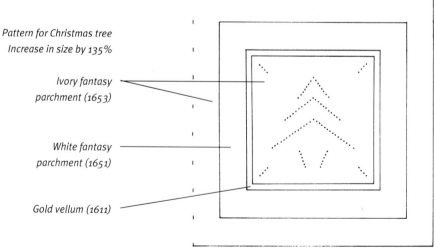

Pattern for Christmas tree
Increase in size by 135%

Ivory fantasy
parchment (1653)

White fantasy
parchment (1651)

Gold vellum (1611)

Star

What you need

- Ivory fantasy parchment (1653)
- White fantasy parchment (1651)
- Gold parchment vellum (1611)
- Sulky thread: gold metallic
- Double-sided adhesive tape

Instructions

General instructions
The card is made from ivory fantasy parchment and has a separating sheet made from white fantasy parchment. The card has three extra sheets stuck on the front. The first extra sheet is made from gold parchment vellum and the second and third extra sheets are made from ivory fantasy parchment. Cut all the pieces to the right size.

Pricking
Prick the pattern in the third extra sheet. Use Perga spray to stick the third extra sheet on the second extra sheet and prick the holes again.

Embroidering
First, embroider the star from the holes in the middle towards the outside and then the lines of the square around the star.

Finishing
Fold the card and use Perga spray to stick the separating sheet behind the front of the card. Use Perga spray to stick the second and third extra sheets on the first extra sheet. Use narrow strips of double-sided adhesive tape to stick this on the card.

Christmas tree

What you need

- *Ivory fantasy parchment (1653)*
- *White fantasy parchment (1651)*
- *Gold parchment vellum (1611)*
- *Sulky thread: gold metallic*
- *Double-sided adhesive tape*

Instructions

General instructions

The card is made from ivory fantasy parchment and has a separating sheet made from white fantasy parchment. The card has three extra sheets stuck on the front. The first extra sheet is made from gold parchment vellum and the second and third extra sheets are made from ivory fantasy parchment. Cut all the pieces to the right size.

Pricking

Prick the pattern in the third extra sheet. Use Perga spray to stick the third extra sheet on the second extra sheet and prick the holes again.

Embroidering

First, embroider the horizontal lines of the Christmas tree. Next, embroider the slanting lines of the Christmas tree and then the lines of the square around the Christmas tree.

Finishing

Fold the card and use Perga spray to stick the separating sheet behind the front of the card. Use Perga spray to stick the second and third extra sheets on the first extra sheet. Use narrow strips of double-sided adhesive tape to stick this on the card.

Thanks to Pergamano International in Uithoorn, the Netherlands. Tel. +31 (0)297 522533, E-mail: info@pergamano.com www.pergamano.com Kars & Co BV in Ochten, the Netherlands. Tel. +31 (0)344 642864